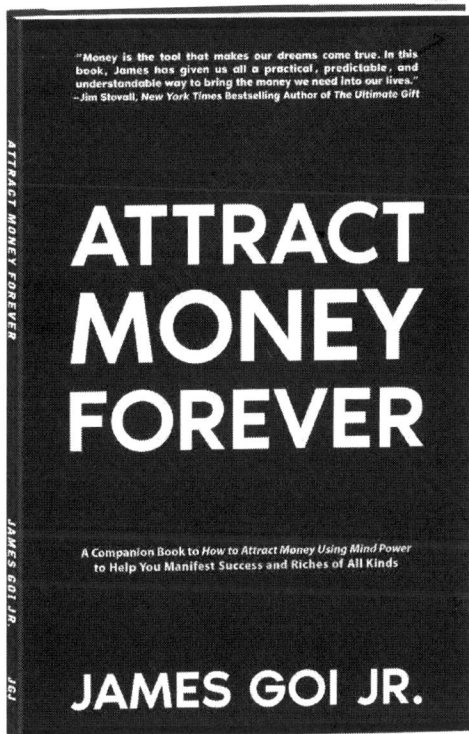

"Money is the tool that makes our dreams come true. In this book, James has given us all a practical, predictable, and understandable way to bring the money we need into our lives."
--Jim Stovall, New York Times Bestselling Author of The Ultimate Gift

ATTRACT MONEY FOREVER

A Companion Book to *How to Attract Money Using Mind Power* to Help You Manifest Success and Riches of All Kinds

JAMES GOI JR.

Attract Money Forever will deepen your understanding of metaphysics and mind-power principles as they relate to attracting money, manifesting abundance, and governing material reality. You'll learn how to use time-tested, time-honored, practical, and spiritual techniques to be more prosperous and improve your life in astounding and meaningful ways. Visit jamesgoijr.com/subscriber-page.html for your free download copy of this amazing book and to receive James's free monthly *Mind Power & Money Ezine*.

SUCCESS
CONSCIOUSNESS

Books by James Goi Jr.

How to Attract Money Using Mind Power
Attract Money Forever
Ten Metaphysical Secrets of Manifesting Money
Advanced Manifesting Made Easy
Aware Power Functioning
The God Function
The Supernatural Power of Thought
Ten Spiritual Secrets of Dead People
Ten Spiritual Secrets of Divine Order
Ten Spiritual Secrets of Thought Power
Self-Defense Techniques and How to Win a Street Fight
The Healing Power of the Light
Spirituality and Metaphysics
Unconditional Love Demystified
Spiritual Power Demystified
Intuition Demystified
Message from the Presence
The True Nature of Reality
Reincarnation and Karma
Vibration and Frequency
Spiritual Understanding
Spiritual Advancement
Spiritual Knowledge
Spiritual Wisdom
Success Consciousness
Higher Consciousness
Light vs. Darkness
The New Normal
My Song Lyrics (multiple volumes)
JGJ Thoughts, Vol. 1

<u>Note</u>

James continues to write new books.
To see the current list, visit his author page at Amazon.com

SUCCESS
CONSCIOUSNESS

252 Inspiring Passages to Help You Reach Your Potential

JAMES GOI JR.

JGJ
JAMES GOI JR.
LA MESA, CALIFORNIA

ISBN:
978-1-68347-071-7 (Trade Paperback)
978-1-68347-072-4 (Kindle)
978-1-68347-073-1 (epub)

Published by:
James Goi Jr.
P.O. Box 563
La Mesa, CA, 91944
www.jamesgoijr.com

PREFACE

Success. Who doesn't want it? Everyone wants to excel, improve, and accomplish in one area of their lives or another. But how to go about it? Most people don't go about seeking success in the most productive ways, and the proof of that statement is that most people never achieve nearly the level of success they would choose for themselves. Far from it, in fact.

So, what's the problem? Well, there are lots of problems. Not the least of which is that people don't develop the proper mindset or *success consciousness* required to achieve their goals in life. If they solve that problem, then they will be able to address the others.

Everything starts in the mind. If the mind is right, everything else will eventually be right as well. You need to understand how your mind works, how the universe works, and how the two interact to create tangible results in our material world.

It's human nature to look for some effortless way to have what we want. But success is not that easy. There are many factors to consider, both tangible and intangible. The only way to figure out the secret to success is to study the subject. And that's where this little book comes in. Read and contemplate the ideas to follow. Let them help you build your own success consciousness, and the life of your dreams.

SUCCESS CONSCIOUSNESS

Without spiritual awareness and a giving spirit, all success rings hollow.

Always strive to think, feel, speak, and act as if the thing you want to bring about is now or will be reality.

Raise your vibration, clarify your vision, manage your mind, and you will attract the needed resources to help speed you along your journey.

There is no paved superhighway to true success. Actually, it's quite a bumpy road.

Growth is success. If you are growing, you are succeeding.

Success is not at the end of the road.
Success *is* the road.

Success is a moving target,
and failure is part of the process.
Just stay in the game, learn as
you go, and you will end up
with something to show.

A strong spiritual foundation is your salvation.
Without it, worldly success rings hollow and
brings sorrow—if not today, tomorrow.

To be successful in life, you'll have to
work with others. Strive to bless the
lives of each and every one of them.
It's not all about you, you know.

More important even than where you go is how you get there.

Reading this quote on success is part of your journey to success. Oh, look right *below* us! There's *another* one!

Success is not about what you look at. It's about how you look at it.

Many average people think success is about fame, fortune, and freedom. Many successful people think success is about passion, purpose, and persistence. And many people just don't think much about success at all. Not surprisingly, many of *those* people are not successful. And surprisingly, some of them *are*.

Success is not a pot of gold at the end of the rainbow. It's picking up pennies in the rain.

Do the right things each day, don't forget to play, be sure to pray, and you will have your way.

You will never be successful until you are successful. You need to be a success before you can be a success. Look in the mirror. Do you see a successful person? If you do, the rest is just details. If you don't see a successful person in the mirror, keep looking until you do.

Do the right things in the right way,
and you will have what you say.

You won't have to give up everything to gain success,
but you will indeed have to give up some things.

More than anything, success is
about what's between your ears
and how you spend your years.

Before you can succeed, you
must dream you can. Then you
must believe in your dream,
which includes believing in
yourself. Get those things
out of the way, and you
are *on* your way.

Enthusiasm for what you want to accomplish will carry you through the darkest days. Without enthusiasm, your dream will sink into the abyss.

Never quit. You can take breaks. Fair enough. But never quit.

The longer it takes you to succeed at your chosen endeavor, the more you will appreciate that success when it comes, and the less likely you will be to take it for granted.

Thank the universe for your struggles and challenges, for without them you could not do much more than remain what you are and where you are.

To realize your personal, unique vision of success, you will have to exercise a fair amount of creativity. You might also be able to succeed by just doing what some other successful person did, without being very creative at all. If you're into that sort of thing, that is...

Add value wherever and whenever you can, keep moving forward, and you won't have to chase success—it will follow you everywhere you go.

Any conversation about success should include a few words about action and work. I wouldn't say they are the most important considerations, but any fool knows you can't leave them out.

Success doesn't happen. *You* do.

Before you start, know *what* and know *why*. Knowing *how* will come later.

Sustained effort guided by acquisition of knowledge and application of intuition will win the day.

There is no substitute for sincerity or passion. Without them, what have you?

If you get to the end of the day having accomplished everything you would have liked to have accomplished that day, you thought too small. That's it.

Can you be happy but not successful? I don't think so. People seek success because they think it will make them happy. If you're already happy, then you are by that definition already successful.

Does your vision of success include the blessing and enrichment of the lives of others? If not, I think you need to rethink your vision of success.

Success is not seized. It is seduced. It is not given. It is gotten.

Be loyal to those you work for, and tolerate nothing less from those who work for you.

You have got to find something you are interested in and just go for it. You have got to answer that which is calling your name.

You know how many people didn't make it from yesterday to today alive? Neither do I, but I'm pretty sure it's a lot. And if you're still alive today, that means there's something for you to do. And if you don't know what it is, you need to figure it out. And once you figure it out, you need to do it. This is not rocket science.

Live every day of your life with the intention of living the last day of your life with as few regrets as possible.

This thing called life was never meant to be easy, but it *was* meant to be fruitful and rewarding. And an easy life could never be either. Don't shy away from the hard work. Expect it, embrace it, and get it done.

Is your environment conducive to success? If not, that would be a good place to start.

There are no mistakes. There are only lessons.

Success is more about what you do with your mind than what you do with your hands. But make no mistake about it—it's about what you do with your hands too.

There is no way around it. Success demands organization. Of *what*? Your thoughts. Your environment. Your schedule. Believe me, we could go on.

It's not going to be easy. In fact, it's going to be downright hard. Strive to remain calm and focused through it all.

A prerequisite for success is the preparation for it.

But where does it all start?
It all starts with desire.

Whatever conditions you seek to create,
strive to make them harmonious.

Nearly every word out of your mouth will affect
someone or something. For the better or the worse.

There is always something
new to learn. And part of that
is learning that some of what
you learned before was not
true. You cannot succeed
without accurate information.

Until you're motivated enough to get motivated, you won't get motivated. So, the first step is to get motivated. And the second step is to get motivated. And the third step is to allow that motivation to propel you forward. And the fourth step is to stay motivated.

It doesn't matter what anyone else thinks. What matters is what *you* think. If you think you can do it, you can probably do it.

To be a success in the eyes of others is great. Sure. But how you feel about it all deep inside determines whether or not you are truly successful.

If you're going to play it big, forget about playing it safe. If you don't believe in what you're doing enough to take the required risks, then you should find something else to do.

If you can't be yourself, what else can you be that will really matter? Don't worry. It's a rhetorical question.

Success is not synonymous with money, but can definitely include it. And the more often, the better. And the more, the merrier.

I confess. I love success.

Seek success not to serve self, but so you can more fully serve others. No, that's not a typo.

Before you are opportunities galore. But you must prepare for them before they appear, recognize them when they do appear, and act on them when they have been recognized. Don't fear a lack of opportunities. Fear a lack of preparation, recognition, and action.

It's not about where you are right now. It's about how far you've come, and how far you want to go.

Don't extract; attract. Don't take; make.

Do not resist failure. The quicker and more often you can fail, the quicker and more often you will succeed. If you knew you'd have to fail 100 times for every one success, you'd be getting those failures out of the way as quickly as possible. Either that, or you'd give up right now. There's always that option too.

It's most often the slow and steady Betty, not the fast and ready Freddy, that wins the marathon of life.

To the best of your ability choose worthwhile tasks to undertake, and give your best to those tasks. Do that and, win or lose, you win.

Do the best you can reasonably do. Become the best you can reasonably become. But don't stress about it. That sucks all the fun out of it.

In the end, all failure is a failure of character. Become a person who cannot fail even when they fail.

What is it you want? Commit yourself to getting it.

When you no longer have goals and aspirations, you will have little reason for getting out of bed in the morning. Always be striving for something. Always be growing in some way. You don't have to be a fanatic about it, but don't be a slouch either.

The longer you are alive, the more you can accomplish while you're here. It's simple math. And the better you take care of yourself physically, mentally, emotionally, and spiritually, the longer you're likely to be alive. It's simple math.

Overcoming challenges is how you grow. The bigger the challenge and subsequent overcoming, the greater the growth. Can that be *bad*?

Success is not what you accomplish next month or next year or ten years from now. Success is what you do each day.

You gotta have a vision. You gotta be committed to it. You gotta keep working toward it. You gotta never give up. What else would you like to know?

Success without discipline does not exist.
Success without discipline is a fluke,
and likely a short-lived one at that.

You might lack many things and still find success
in your chosen game. But if you lack the will to do
what it takes to win, you might as well not even play.

Success is relative. Failure is
relative. Just take a good look
at your relatives, and you'll see
the truth of what I'm saying.

With all this talk of success, let me slip in here a quick reminder,
warning, and caveat: If your definition of success will cause undue
harm or loss to others, there will one day be a steep price to pay.

Unless you're doing something that really matters,
nothing else you're doing really matters.

Success requires both risk taking and caution. It's a delicate balance which requires constant diligence to maintain.

If you do not have a strong spiritual foundation under your material success, don't get too comfortable just yet.

For practical purposes, the bottom line is that you are successful if you think you are successful.

It's not about how much time it takes. It's about how you take the time.

There are certain monetary realities involved in modern life. Keep that in mind while planning your future success. You don't have to live in a mansion, but neither do you want to be living under a bridge. At least I *hope* you don't.

If you need to compare yourself to others to determine how successful you are, don't bother. Compare yourself to what you used to be.

Competition can bring out the best in human beings. Competition can bring out the worst in human beings. In the end, it's not really about winning or losing. It's about how you played the game, and what you became in the process.

Honesty. Accept no substitute. From yourself or others.

Do what you love doing, even if you have to do something you don't love doing to be able to do what you love doing, and it's a fair bet that over time you'll be able to do more of the one and less of the other. Do what you don't love doing so that someday you'll be able to do what you love doing, and it's a fair bet that such a day will never come.

Think, feel, speak, and act as if you are already a success. Do that, and the facts to back up your thoughts, feelings, words, and actions will not be far behind.

Little things
make a big difference.

You have to be clear on what you want, and go after it with a determination the universe cannot ignore.

To succeed in any endeavor, you can't get around the fact that you've got to develop the proper attitude.

To attract good fortune, start by being good.

Toward the end of your life, when you're looking back on it, one of the most rewarding things you can know is that at least parts of the world and at least some of its people are better off because you lived.

Every single day is an opportunity to be better and do better than the day before. Every single day.
Do you really *get* that?

Success comes easy to those who work hard at it.

Prepare yourself for success by being worthy of receiving it, capable of handling it, and desirous of sharing it.

The higher you want to build your success, the stronger must be your foundation.

He who is a nice person is already a success regardless of his bank account or social standing.

Ability is helpful. Attitude is crucial.

Giving more than you take is a key ingredient in true success.

In the end it's really not about what you do, it's about what you become in the process.

There are so many things that are beyond your individual control. And you likely comprehend that. But there are likely more things that could be within your individual control than you have ever dreamed.

No one has ever been truly rich who has come to the end of their life spiritually poor.

If you are still alive, then technically speaking you are succeeding at living. Now that you've got that out of the way, what else can you take on?

Success is mostly about how you measure it.

Love, compassion, kindness, fairness, loyalty, goodwill... These are the characteristics of a person succeeding at being a decent human being.

The sun rises. The sun sets. The tide comes in. The tide goes out. Success comes. Success goes. What remains is the experiencer of it all.

Immerse yourself in the study of that which most interests you, and express what you learn in ways worthy of study by others.

No matter how high you go, strive to remain grounded.

The main work of success is preparing for it.

Success! Feel it!

You can't very well advance toward your future while obsessing over your past.

Today is a new day. It will be what you make of it. Sure, there are a lot of obstacles to your success. But so what?

Measure your success not by how many dollars you have accumulated, but by how many people you have benefited.

If you are not doing what you love, then you are not a success no matter how much of a success you are. Let me repeat that.

Do you *have* to work each working day, or do you *get* to work each working day? There is a world of difference between the two, you know.

If you are different, they may recoil a bit at first. But don't you worry. Keep doing your thing. If it's a thing worth doing, they'll likely come around. But be true to yourself no matter what.

If your success costs you your health or peace of mind, you have failed at success.

Concentrate, innovate, and demonstrate.

Ongoing success requires constant adaptation. What worked yesterday might not work today. What works today might not work tomorrow.

Determination gives knowledge a good run for its money up the ladder of success. Just look at all the successful people who really don't know what the heck they're doing.

Focus on your strengths, strengthen your weaknesses, guard your time, and keep working toward your goals. Then rest, relax, and sleep. Then wake up, get out of bed, and do it all again.

There is only so much time in each day.
How much of it are you comfortable wasting?

Just one hour a day intensely focused on what you most want to accomplish in your life adds up to more than nine forty-hour work weeks at the end of the year! And what about *two* hours a day? This is getting *exciting*!

Talent is a strong competitor, but tenacity gives it a run for its money. And when the two come together? Well, you can imagine.

You won't automatically become a different person once you reach a huge goal. But you will incrementally become a different person all along the way.

Money is not the most important thing, but it sure can buy a lot of important things.

Do what you do best with zest, and hire others to do the rest at your behest.

All the good that comes to you will come from the universe, and much of that through other people. Don't take either for granted, and treat each with the respect and consideration they deserve.

You cannot bargain or haggle for success. Its price is non-negotiable.

There's nothing big. There's just a bunch of little things added up.

Never forget this: what you own can own *you* as well.

Do what you love doing. Start there. You'll figure out the rest.

To the unknowing, success is mostly what can be seen with the eyes. To the knowing, success is mostly what can only be seen with the heart.

Trying to be successful while resenting successful people is like trying to breathe underwater.

Confidence: Good. Arrogance: Not so good.

The pursuit of worldly success has been and continues to be the moral downfall of many. It's better to be an honest baker than a dishonest banker.

If you come up with something really new, don't expect everyone to sing your praises. In fact, in the beginning, expect just the opposite.

Luck is not something that happens to you. It's something you make happen.

Give your first and best energy and focus to
the spiritual side of life, then what's left
to the material side. Remember, the
horse always comes before the cart.

Why do you want what you want?
It's one of the most important
questions you can ask yourself.

You will accomplish what you accomplish by
the grace of a power much greater than you.

People are what life is about.
Any true success must include
success with people.

If you are successful at wielding power in harmful ways, you have succeeded at sealing your own fate. And it will be worse than that of those you harmed.

Your success will require you to work with other people in various ways and at various times. Remotely. In person. Whatever. Always strive to leave the other person feeling good about their interaction with you.

Work for the greater good of humanity, and you will have all creation rooting for you and pulling strings on your behalf.

Why race to escape circumstances you'll one day be nostalgic for? Slow down. Enjoy the journey.

Desire and enthusiasm are great, but they should be mixed with equal parts of contemplation and common sense.

The problem with most people seeking success is that they are going by someone else's definition of success. So if and when they succeed, they discover they've failed. Then if they still have any steam left in them—it's back to the drawing board.

To succeed without violating your conscience is the trick. Anything else is surrender and defeat.

It will be a sad day if you ever reach
the highest peak. For from there,
the only place left to go is down.

Today's word is *industrious*,
which means to be diligent
and hardworking. Without
that, what have you got?

You'll get there when you're ready to be there.
And if you get there any sooner,
you might not be there very long.

By trial and error, you become
more competent and confident.

Don't expect other people to rejoice in your success. Quite the contrary, many would rejoice in your downfall.

If you gave it your all and never quit, you have succeeded regardless of the outcome.

Put everything you are into everything you do. Anything less, and you're just another kid from the neighborhood.

Regret and sadness await those who fritter away their days.

Improvement is a good thing.
Self-improvement is a *great* thing.

You should learn something from
every mistake. Every failure should
bring you another step closer to success.

If you are consistent in your
efforts, you will accomplish
things. What you are consistent
at doing will determine what you
accomplish. And that can be a
good thing or a bad thing.

Never underestimate the power
of a positive mental attitude.

Many set out for success having only a vague idea of what it will be like if they reach their goal. And most of that vague idea is the desirable part of the equation. But it's OK. They'll learn about the other stuff when they reach their goal. And if they don't reach their goal, it's a moot point anyway.

Overindulgence in the fruits of success is a sure way to chop down that tree.

Most of what you'll learn is all the things that don't work. But that's OK. You only need to know a few things that do.

Success without peace of mind is like a sunrise without the sun.

Ultimately, the process of turning immaterial dreams into material results is a spiritual process. As is everything else in life. The better you come to understand that, the more at peace you will be and the more harmonious conditions and circumstances you will create.

Even a recluse can attain worldly success. But he or she will have to poke their head out of that cave every once in a while.

Set up the space for others to be successful, and you enlarge your own space for doing so.

Don't let your success go to your head. And don't let your head go to failure.

Wake up each day knowing anything is possible. Go to bed each night knowing you did what you could do, and tomorrow you get another go at it.

You don't have to be king or queen of the world, or even mayor of your little town or owner of the business you work at. If you have what you need, if you are making a positive contribution, if you enjoy what you are doing, and if you are happy, then you are indeed successful and a member of an exclusive club.

I think some super-successful people have determined the American Dream is actually a nightmare. But *now* what are they supposed to do?

For most people to succeed will require a major attitude adjustment. I won't say attitude is everything, but it's pretty darn important.

Positive thinking, mind power, and all that sort of thing. Is it really even all that important? If you have to ask the question, you might not understand the answer.

Try to give more than you get. I dare you.

There really is no success or failure. There is only what is, and how we interpret it.

No matter what anyone else ever said or did, or didn't say or do, your current place in life is not on them. It's on you. Accepting full responsibility for your life will put you in the best possible position to be able to transform your life into what you dream it can be.

It's fine to dream of success, but eventually you'll have to wake up and make that dream come true.

Vision shows you *where* you're going. Motivation *gets* you going. Persistence *keeps* you going.

Gratitude for what you have will attract more of what you are grateful for into your life. I know it sounds too easy to be true. Still, there it is.

Failures are the steps on the stairway to success. And each success is a landing from which you can see more clearly the next flight of stairs.

Working in harmony with others toward positive, shared goals creates a magical force that the universe recognizes and supports.

Constant adaptation is the way to stay safe and successful.

More of a blessing than even the success itself is the opportunity to be able to earn it.

Don't spend your life trying to duplicate others. Spend your life trying to authenticate yourself.

How you start out each morning sets the tone for the rest of the day. When you awaken, check your attitude. If it's not right, don't step out of that bed until it is.

The habit of never *giving* up is one that will *carry* you up.

Anyone can dream. But a dream is just a dream until you dedicate yourself to making it come true. Don't think, *that would be nice.* Instead think, *that will be period.*

The more you help others, the more you help yourself. Yes, people can become "successful" by taking advantage of other people instead of helping them. But success is about more than fame, fortune, power, and self. If you already knew that, you didn't need to read this. And if you didn't already know that, it likely won't matter that you *did* read this. So come to think of it, I'm not even sure why I *wrote* it!

Should you be running away from where you are, or running toward where you're going? Think. Can you do one without doing the other?

Self-discipline leads to the formation of new habits of thought, feeling, and action. And new habits of thought, feeling, and action make self-discipline of thought, feeling, and action less necessary. In other words, it requires more effort to get your life going in a new direction than it does to keep your life going in that new direction.

Success is not the goal. Success is the result of achieving the goal. That is, if the goal is worth achieving.

Success is born of a dream, and grown by action.

If you routinely get bored, then you haven't yet figured out the purpose of your life. Once you discover the purpose of your life, you'll be so busy working at fulfilling it that you'll have no time to be bored.

No matter what anyone else says, you are worthy of the success you seek. If you don't know that, any success you gain is likely to be hard-won and easily lost. Come to think of it, though, even if you know you are worthy of success, it's still probably going to be hard-won. But that's beside the point.

You have got to stay focused, and you have got to find some way to devote your best energy to reaching your goals—day after day after ever-lovin' day.

Success is serving a useful purpose, being happy and content in the process, keeping a roof you like over your head and food of your choice on the table, and having the time to do the things you enjoy doing. We don't need to make this any more complicated than that.

The universe has a place for you, and tasks it wants you to do. And the universe is forever trying to nudge you in that direction. Through contemplation and self-reflection, you can begin to know what the universe is trying to tell you. And once you do, everything will start to make sense.

There is one simple habit that perhaps above all others will help guide you in the direction of your ultimate success in all endeavors large and small. And that is the habit of following your intuition. You have within you an infallible guidance system. Follow it, and all will be well.

Success is less about what you do on the sunny days, and more about what you do on the rainy days.

You exist within a field of malleable energy that is subject to your will and intention. No matter how powerful you think you are, you have barely any idea of how powerful you actually are. And you can use your power for good or for bad. Use it for good, and the universe will lift you up and pat you on the back. Use it for bad, and the universe will knock you down and kick you in the butt.

Sincere gratitude for everything in your life regardless of whether you think it's good or bad will attract to you more of what you think is good and less of what you think is bad. And if you are continually attracting to you more of what you think is good and less of what you think is bad, you are by definition in the process of living a successful life.

By cutting corners, you are cheating yourself and everyone else. You are either serious and conscientious about what you are doing, or you're not. In the long run you'll find, though, you really never get away with anything.

Health is wealth. But wealth is not always health.

You strive for success so you can be comfortable. But once you are comfortably enjoying your success, be careful not to become too comfortable. If you do, you might find that things get uncomfortable again.

Look around you. Are the people, places, and activities you involve yourself with supporting your efforts to move forward? If not, then they are keeping you from moving forward. There are no neutral people, places, or activities. Everything affects everything.

Spiritual strength fosters mental strength. Mental strength fosters emotional strength. And to be strong spiritually, mentally, and emotionally is to be truly strong. And if you are truly strong, you are a force to be reckoned with.

If you are steadily advancing toward a worthwhile goal you have chosen for yourself, all is well. It doesn't matter how long you've been at it. It doesn't matter how old you are. If you're getting further, and your goal is getting closer, then just keep on going. There is no viable alternative.

Affirmation, visualization, acting as if, positive thinking. That might be an incomplete sentence, but so what? You get the idea.

Don't wonder if you can keep pushing forward.
You can. Perhaps all you need is a good night's sleep.

If you believe deep down in your heart that the thing you are being called to do is the thing you should be doing, then come what may, do it.

You need to use your head to find success, but don't let success go to your head once you do find it.

Don't run out of steam before you reach your dream. It might be just around the next bend.

Never pursue a goal at any cost. If you do, you'll likely end up compromising your moral standards somewhere along the way. And once you've been at it for a while, never be afraid to reconsider your goal. Perhaps the universe has been blocking you from having it—for your own highest best good. Perhaps you don't even really want it all that much any longer. If you still think it's right for you, though, fine, go for it. But always remember there's no shame in changing your mind and abandoning one goal for another. Better to quit now than to accomplish the thing and wish you hadn't. Anyway, don't be a robot. That's my point.

Use common sense, critical thinking, and intuition all along the way.

You don't have to get it perfect to claim success. In fact, you don't have to get it perfect at all. But for sure you want to get it good or even great.

Success won't make you a good person. And it won't make you a bad person. It will just make it more apparent to more people which of the two you are.

If you work with the laws of the universe, you will find your path prepared for you as you move down it. And if you want to work with the laws of the universe, you can do no better thing than to learn some spiritual and metaphysical techniques and to practice them every day in all areas of your life.

It's not enough to have a big dream. You'll have to attend to an infinite number of small details.

Success is not just about working hard. You've got to work on the right things in the right ways at the right times for the right reasons.

Success is more a mindset than an outcome.
And with the right mindset, you'll get the right outcomes.

Success without a plan is not likely.
You can modify your plan as needed,
but you should indeed have one.

Willpower to both do things
you don't want to do and not
do things you do want to do
will carry you far down the
road to success. It's not all you
need, but without it there
is not much hope for you.

There is a recipe for success, just like
for any culinary creation. Both have
room for personalization. But only so
much. There are certain ingredients
that simply cannot be left out.

Success without failure is impossible.
Failure without success is unthinkable.

If society deems you a success but there is still a void in your soul, you've still got some things to figure out and some work to do. You can fool other people indefinitely, but you can fool yourself for only so long.

You can fail your way to success, or succeed your way to failure. The choice is yours.

Massive action may be the way to massive success, but you should be pretty sure that where you are heading is really where you want to go and a place worth being.

Success comes, and success goes. Failure comes, and failure goes. I wouldn't get all worked up about it either way. Just stay calm, and carry on.

The masses both love and hate successful people. They just can't seem to make up their minds on the issue.

Be kind and fair with everyone, and you are succeeding at being a decent human being. And if you are not succeeding at being a decent human being, then it really won't matter all that much what else you are succeeding at.

If you end up alone in your success, you've actually failed. Your success is nothing if you have no one to share it with.

Whatever the work is, try to work with people who care about it as much as you do—or at least as close to that as possible.

Have a plan, show up on time, work like the dickens, take some breaks, keep a positive attitude, keep learning, be nice to the people you meet, and take care of your health. That's what I can think of at the moment. I think it's a pretty good start.

If you get to do what you love every day, you are already a success. Don't worry about what your mother-in-law has to say about it. Of course, if she does bring up the subject, be very cordial and pleasant about the whole thing. You never know, you might be needing to borrow some money from her one of these days.

You'll wonder if it's all really even worth it, and you'll need to realize it most certainly is.

One day I learned that success is sometimes attained by people who don't know what the heck they're doing. It was on that day I realized I too could one day be successful.

I shouldn't have to say this, but only work toward goals that are good, honest, just, and that will not cause any undue harm or loss to others.

Success doesn't happen overnight. Success doesn't always happen over decade. As long as it happens over lifetime, you're good.

If you're unhappy now, you'll likely be unhappy if and when you find the success you are seeking. If you're happy now, you'll likely be happy if and when you find the success you are seeking. Same success. Different person.

Your homelife is more important than you might think. It affects much of what you do and how you are when you're away from your home. So give your homelife the attention it deserves. It should be orderly, peaceful, relaxing, and pleasant. Success starts at home.

You must believe in what you are doing, and do what you believe in.

Some people avoid success because they fear it might cause them to lose what they have. But they don't have anything. Can someone please explain that one to me?

If you don't enjoy your journey to success, you're not likely to enjoy your success much either. And if you enjoy your journey to success, you're already a success!

Continually improve, bit by bit. On *what*?
On *everything*. Starting with *you*.

Before you set out to build your empire,
get your own house in order.

Desire will motivate you, but without persistence your motivation will wane and your desire will fade.

No matter what happens, keep your sense of humor about it. We're all going to end up in a box or a furnace at the end anyway.

Light a match, use your lighter, rub two sticks together, whatever the heck you have to do to get that fire going. Then feed and fan those flames like nobody's business for the rest of your life.

What good is it to be a success on the stage if you are a failure behind the curtain?

What you create will come and go, but what you become in the process will remain.

Always remember, the success you seek is inside you. There is really nothing out *there*. Ultimately, the road to success is the road to self-discovery.

AFTERWORD

Thank you for reading this book. I hope you have enjoyed it. And I hope you will continue to benefit from having read it. I have benefited greatly from having read countless books over the years.

I began to find my first self-help, spiritual, and metaphysical books in my early twenties, not long after I moved from New Jersey to California to try to find my way in the world. Before that move, I had no idea such books even existed.

And honestly, were it not for such books and my intense desire to learn, to grow, and to improve myself and my circumstances, I would have gone down a completely different road in life—a road I would rather not even think about or imagine.

Who could deny the assertion that books can and do change lives? It is my mission to write some of those books that do indeed change lives. I want people's lives to be better because I lived and because I wrote.

There are reasons I came into this life, and writing is one of them. I am living the life I was meant to live, and it is my sincere desire that you will live the life you were meant to live.

Can I ask two favors of you? First, if you think this or any of my other books can help people in some of the ways they could use help, will you help spread the word about me and my writings? You could do that by loaning my books to others, giving my books as gifts, and by telling people about my books and about me. By doing these things, you will bless me beyond measure, and I truly believe you will bless others beyond measure as well.

Second, please consider writing an honest review for this book. Doing so will help other readers decide whether or not the book might be right for them. And keep in mind that a review does not have to be long. Even just a few words or a sentence or two could be sufficient. And if you do not feel inclined to write a review at all, you can simply click on a star rating to rate the book and still have your voice heard.

Finally, always remember, you are capable of so much more than you have ever imagined. Learn, believe, act, and persist. Do those four things, and nothing will stop you from continuing to build a better and better life for yourself and for those you care about.

Peace & Plenty . . .

ABOUT THE AUTHOR

James Goi Jr., aka The Attract Money Guru™, is the bestselling author of the internationally published *How to Attract Money Using Mind Power*, a book that set a new standard for concise, no-nonsense, straight-to-the-point self-help books. First published in 2007, that game-changing book continues to transform lives around the world. And though it would be years before James would write new books, and even more years before he would publish new books, that first book set the tone for his writing career. The tagline for James as an author and publisher is Books to Awaken, Uplift, and Empower™. And James takes those words seriously, as is evident in every book he writes. James: is a relative recluse and spends most of his time alone; is an advanced mind-power practitioner, a natural-born astral traveler, and an experienced lucid dreamer; has had life-changing encounters with both angels and demons, and even sees some dead people; has been the grateful recipient of an inordinate amount of life-saving divine intervention; is a poet and songwriter; is a genuinely nice guy who cares about people and all forms of life; fasts regularly; is a sincere seeker of higher human health; is an objective observer, a persistent ponderer, and a deliberate deducer; and has a supple sense of heady humor.

STAY IN TOUCH WITH JAMES

If you are a sincere seeker of spiritual truth and/or a determined pursuer of material wealth and success, James could be the lifeline and the go-to resource you have been hoping to find. Step One, subscribe to James's free monthly *Mind Power & Money Ezine* here: jamesgoijr.com/subscriber-page.html. Step Two, connect with James online anywhere and everywhere you can find him. You can start here:

Facebook.com/JamesGoiJr
Facebook.com/JamesGoiJrPublicPage
Facbook.com/HowToAttractMoneyUsingMindPower
Twitter.com/JamesGoiJr
Linkedin.com/in/JamesGoiJr
Pinterest.com/JamesGoiJr
Youtube.com/JamesGoiJr
Instagram.com/JamesGoiJr
Goodreads.com/JamesGoiJr
jamesgoijr.tumblr.com

James' Amazon Author Page

A great resource to help you keep abreast of James's ever-expanding list of books is his author page at Amazon.com. There you will find all of his published writings and have easy access to them in the various editions in which they will be published.

Suggested for You

From time to time, James comes across products he thinks might be of interest to his readers, and he posts the links to those products on his website. To see what might be currently listed, visit that page here: jamesgoijr.com/suggested.html

SPECIAL ACKNOWLEDGEMENT

To Kathy Darlene Hunt, who has been my rock, my Light, my safety net, and my buffer since I was in my twenties. She rightfully shares in the credit for every book I've written, for the books I'm working on now, and for every single book I will ever write.

Kathy Darlene Hunt
Author of *A Child of the Light*
jamesgoijr.com/kdh.html

A FREE GIFT FOR YOU!

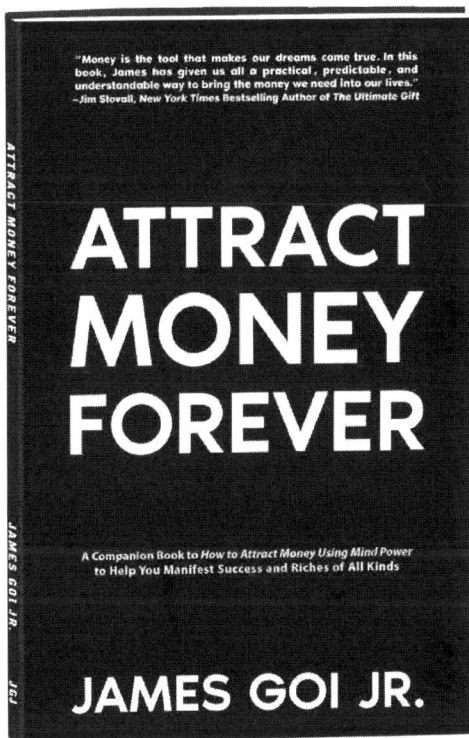

Attract Money Forever will deepen your understanding of metaphysics and mind-power principles as they relate to attracting money, manifesting abundance, and governing material reality. You'll learn how to use time-tested, time-honored, practical, and spiritual techniques to be more prosperous and improve your life in astounding and meaningful ways. Visit jamesgoijr.com/subscriber-page.html for your free download copy of this amazing book and to receive James's free monthly *Mind Power & Money Ezine*.

FURTHER READING

10 Secrets for Success and Inner Peace by Dr. Wayne W. Dyer

100 Things Successful People Do by Nigel Cumberland

The 10X Rule by Grant Cardone

12 Concepts of Success by Dr. Ivan W. Perkinson

The 25 Biblical Laws of Success by William Douglas and Rubens Teixeira

The ABCs of Success by Bob Proctor

Abundance Now by Lisa Nichols and Janet Switzer

Act Like a Success, Think Like a Success by Steve Harvey

The Amazing Power of Deliberate Intent by Esther Hicks and Jerry Hicks

As a Man Thinketh by James Allen

Awakened Imagination by Neville Goddard

The Awakened Millionaire by Joe Vitale

Awaken the Giant Within by Tony Robbins

The Biology of Belief by Bruce H. Lipton, Ph.D.

The Charge by Brendon Burchard

Clarity by Jamie Smart

The Compound Effect by Darren Hardy

The Cosmic Code by Heinz R. Pagels

The Cosmic Ordering Service by Barbel Mohr

Create Your Own Future by Brian Tracy

Creative Visualization by Shakti Gawain

The Dancing Wu Li Masters by Gary Zukav

The Diamond in Your Pocket by Gangaji

The Dice Game of Shiva by Richard Smoley

Divine Audacity by Linda Martella-Whitsett

The Divine Matrix by Gregg Braden

Dreamed Up Reality by Dr. Bernardo Kastrup

Emergence by Derek Rydall

The Field by Lynne McTaggart
Fit For Success by Nick Shaw
Follow Your Passion, Find Your Power by Bob Doyle
The Four Desires by Rod Stryker
Frequency by Penney Peirce
Having It All by John Assaraf
The Hidden Power by Thomas Troward
How Successful People Think by John C. Maxwell
I AM by Vivian E. Amis
I Wish I Knew This 20 Years Ago by Justin Perry
Infinite Potential by Lothar Schafer
Instant Motivation by Chantal Burns
It Works by RHJ
Just Ask the Universe by Michael Samuels
Key to Yourself by Venice J. Bloodworth
The Keys to Success by Jim Rohn
The Law of Agreement by Tony Burroghs
The Law of Success by Napoleon Hill
Lessons in Truth by H. Emilie Cady
Life Power and How to Use It by Elizabeth Towne
Life Visioning by Michael Bernard Beckwith
Live Your Dreams by Les Brown
The Magic Lamp by Keith Ellis
The Magic of Believing by Claude M. Bristol
The Magic of Thinking Big by David J. Schwartz
Make Magic of Your Life by T. Thorne Coyle
Manifesting Change by Mike Dooley
The Map by Boni Lonnsburry
The Master Key System by Charles F. Haanel
The Millionaire Mind by Thomas J. Stanley
Millionaire Success Habits by Dean Graziosi
Mind and Success by W. Ellis Williams
Mind into Matter by Fred Alan Wolf, Ph.D.
Mind Power into the 21st Century by John Kehoe
Mindset by Carol S. Dweck
Miracles by Stuart Wilde

The Miracles in You by Mark Victor Hansen and Ben Carson (Foreword)

Mysticism and the New Physics by Michael Talbot

New Physics and the Mind by Robert Paster

Nine Things Successful People Do Differently by Heidi Grant Halvorson

The One Command by Asara Lovejoy

One Mind by Larry Dossey, M.D.

The One Thing by Garry Keller with Jay Papasan

One Simple Idea by Mitch Horowitz

Our Invisible Supply by Frances Larimer Warner

Physics on the Fringe by Margaret Wertheim

Playing the Quantum Field by Brenda Anderson

The Power of Now by Eckhart Tolle

The Power of Positive Thinking by Dr. Norman Vincent Peale

The Power of Your Subconscious Mind by Joseph Murphy

The Power to Get Things Done by Steve Levinson Ph.D. and Chris Cooper

Programming the Universe by Seth Lloyd

Prosperity by Charles Fillmore

Psycho-Cybernetics by Maxwell Maltz

Quantum Creativity by Pamela Meyer

Quantum Jumps by Cynthia Sue Larson

Quantum Reality by Nick Herbert

The Quantum Self by Danah Zohar

Quantum Success by Sandra Anne Taylor

Reality Creation 101 by Christopher A. Pinckley

Reality Unveiled by Ziad Masri

Rhinoceros Success by Scott Alexander

The School of Greatness by Lewis Howes

The Science Behind Success by Jayson Krause

The Science of Getting Rich by Wallace D. Wattles

The Science of Mind by Ernest Holmes

The Secret by Rhonda Byrne

The Secret of the Ages by Robert Collier
See You at the Top by Zig Ziglar
The Self-Aware Universe by Amit Goswami
The Seven Spiritual Laws of Success by Deepak Chopra
Shadows of the Mind by Roger Penrose
Shift Your Mind by Steve Chandler
The Slight Edge by Jeff Olson
Soul Purpose by Mark Thurstan, Ph.D.
Spiritual Economics by Eric Butterworth
The Success Factor by Ruth Gotian
Success Is for You by Dr. David R. Hawkins
Success Is Not an Accident by Tommy Newberry
The Success Principles by Jack Canfield
Success Through Subconscious Mastery by Ausra Cerniauskiene
Supreme Influence by Niurka
Thought Power by Annie Besant
Thoughts Are Things by Prentice Mulford
Train Your Mind To Be Successful by Sayra Montes
True Purpose by Tim Kelley
True Spirituality & the Law of Attraction by Karl W. Gruber
The Twelve Universal Laws of Success by Herbert Harris
The Universe Is a Dream by Alexander Marchand
Unleash Your Full Potential by James Rick
Unreasonable Success and How to Achieve It by Richard Koch
Warped Passages by Lisa Randall
What Is Self? by Bernadette Roberts
Working with the Law by Raymond Holliwell
You Are the World by Jiddu Krishnamurti
Your Invisible Power by Genevieve Behrend
You Unlimited by Norman S. Lunde
The Zigzag Principle by Rich Christiansen